BUBBLE BUTT!

The Challenged Sea Turtle Of The Mystic Aquarium

Written by
KIKI LATIMER

Illustrated by
BUNNY GRIFFETH

Author: Kiki Latimer
Illustrator: Bunny Griffeth
Page layout: Louise Canuto
© Copyright 2010, Educa Vision Inc.
Coconut Creek, FL

Educa Vision Inc.,
7550 NW 47th Avenue
Coconut Creek, FL 33073
Tel: 954-968-7433
Fax: 954-970-0330
Web: www.educavision.com

ISBN10: 1-58432-637-9
ISBN13: 978-1-58432-637-3

Special Thanks
to
The Georgia Sea Turtle Center
Jekyll Island, Georgia
and
The Mystic Aquarium & Institute for Exploration
Mystic, Connecticutt

Dedicated
to
Adam MacKinnon
and to
Cameron, Jonathon, Joshua, and Jaedon

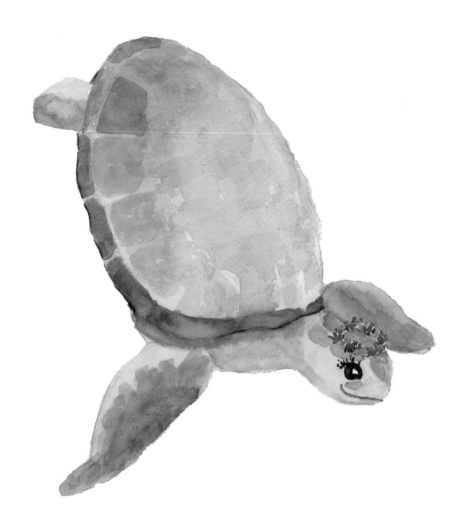

Once upon a time in the sea!
Once upon a time in the sea!
Lived a turtle shy and sweet,
The kind you'd like to meet
If you were a creature swimming by!

This was Charlotte the sea turtle!
This was Charlotte the sea turtle!
She'd dance through a wave,
She was gentle, kind, and brave
And happy that her name wasn't Myrtle!

Now, Charlotte was no ordinary creature!
No, Charlotte was no ordinary creature!
She would give a little wink
Just to try and make you think!
She hoped one day that she would be a teacher!

So Charlotte often had her nose in a book.
Yes, Charlotte had her nose in a book!
Charlotte loved to read
While she chewed upon seaweed!
She loved Moby Dick and Captain Hook!

Now Charlotte read a book every day.
Yes, Charlotte read a book every day!
With every page she'd turn
Something fun and new she'd learn!
A smarter turtle never came your way!

Moby Dick

But Charlotte's story had a simple plot.
Yes, Charlotte's story had a simple plot.
She thought she'd always be
A turtle in the sea,
Then a boat propeller changed things a lot.

One day she was swimming through the waters!
Yes, one day she was swimming through the waters!
She saw a boat going fast!
As it suddenly went past
Charlotte felt it hit her hindquarters.

Charlotte was a turtle of the deep blue sea!
Charlotte was a turtle of the deep blue sea!
Then this boat gave her a bump
Made a boo-boo on her rump
She washed up on the beach by a tree.

15

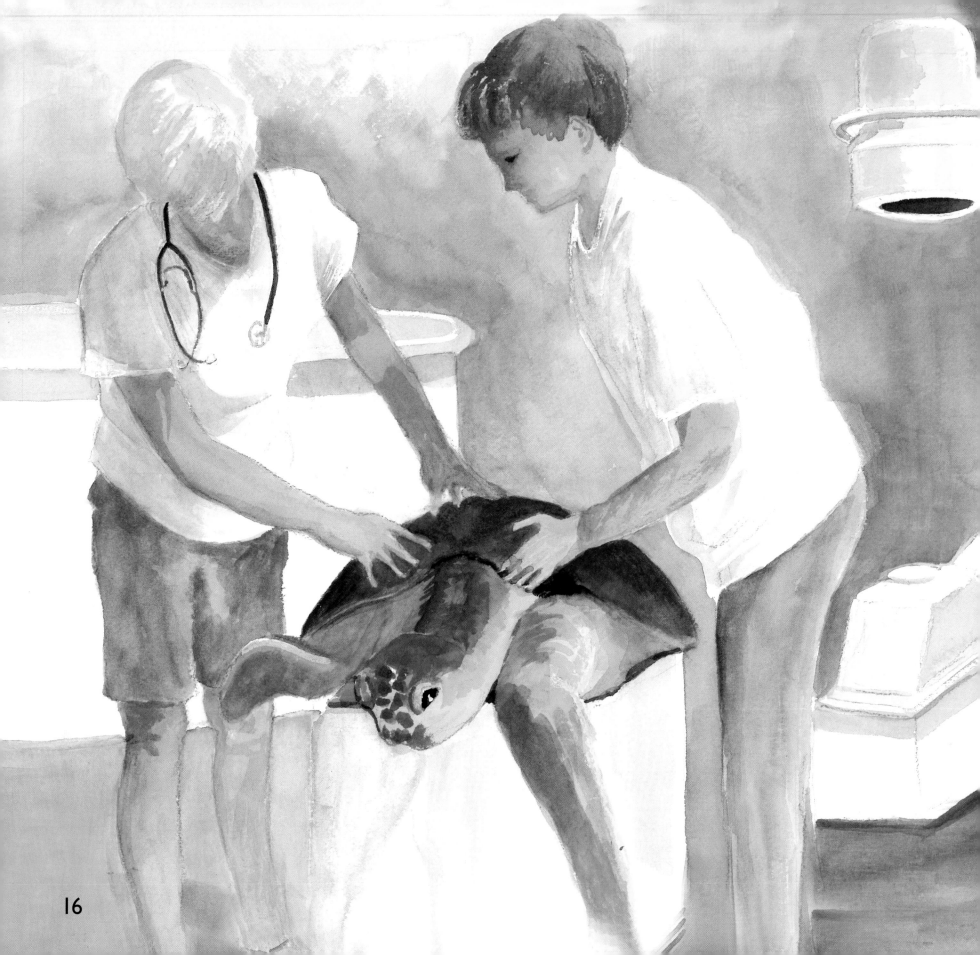

Well, Charlotte was rushed to the doctor and the nurse!
Yes, Charlotte was rushed to the doctor and the nurse!
They x-rayed Charlotte's hiney
She was feeling sad and whiney
But they made sure she didn't get much worse.

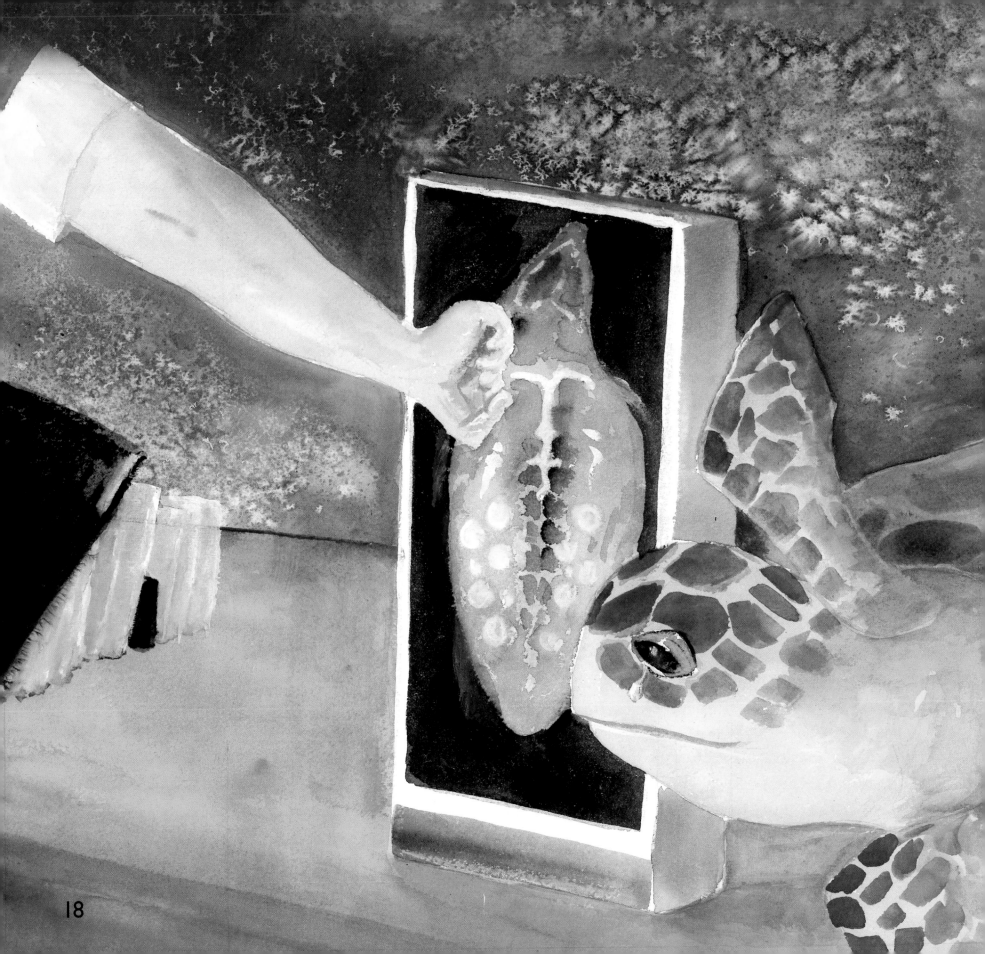

Now Charlotte was a turtle
with some troubles!
Yes, Charlotte was a turtle
with some troubles!
She had a belly ache
And some medicine
she must take
'Cause now she had
a tummy full of bubbles!

Yes, Charlotte had these bubbles in her belly!
Yes, Charlotte had these bubbles in her belly!
Then they moved to her butt
And that's where they got stuck
Now her bum floats like a fish made out of jelly!

The bubbles in Charlotte's bum
were there to stay!
Yes, the bubbles in Charlotte's bum
were there to stay!
Now too slow to catch her lunch
She would have to learn to munch
On whatever came her way
throughout the day!

Now Charlotte would not be safe in the ocean!
No, Charlotte would not be safe in the ocean.
She could turn out to be lunch
For someone else to munch!
She really didn't care for this notion!

So Charlotte waved goodbye to the sea!
Yes, Charlotte waved goodbye to the sea!

It was a moment very sad
Then it began to make her mad!
So she sent for a nice hot cup of tea!

Now Charlotte sipped her tea in a fit.
Yes, Charlotte sipped her tea in a fit.
Then she blew her runny nose,
As she thought about her woes,
And she cried about her bum being hit.

Then Charlotte said "Enough is enough!"
Yes, Charlotte said "Enough is enough!"
Then she slurped down the last sip of tea.
And she said "I am still me!"
She was made of the right kind of stuff!

For Charlotte was a tough young turtle!
Yes, Charlotte was a tough young turtle!
Through these waters she'd sail!
There was no way she'd fail.
She would find her way past this rough hurdle!

And well, Charlotte rather liked her bubble behind!
Yes, Charlotte rather liked her bubble behind!
It made her different from the rest
Put her courage to the test
From it a new life she would find!

In Mystic was an aquarium like the sea!
Yes, in Mystic was an aquarium like the sea!
Charlotte sent her resume
Then she wondered night and day
If with lions of the sea she would be.

Mystic said Yes! She could come!
Mystic said Yes! She could come!
If the sting rays didn't throw a tantrum!
So Charlotte moved into their tank,
And they found her rather swank.
They didn't even mind her bubble bum!

Now Charlotte swims around like the queen!
Yes, Charlotte swims around like the queen!
She's as happy as can be
As anyone there can see!
So making fun of her butt would be mean!

Besides, our Charlotte is a turtle rather rare!
Yes, our Charlotte is a turtle rather rare!
And she just might make you wish
You were a turtle or a fish
With bubbles in your own derriere!

So we laugh with Charlotte and we see!
Yes, we laugh with Charlotte and we see!
That she's become a teacher
For every sort of creature
Including the likes of you and me!

34

For Charlotte teaches us to understand!
Yes, Charlotte teaches us to understand
That the creatures of the sea
May need help from you and me!
Our hearts are where the ocean meets the land!

Charlotte was a turtle of the deep blue sea!
Charlotte was a turtle of the deep blue sea!
Then that boat gave her a bump
Made a boo-boo on her rump
Now she's a friend for you and me!

So when you visit Charlotte bring a book!
Yes, when you visit Charlotte bring a book!
Hold it up for her to see!
So delighted she'll be!
She might even nod hi! and take a look!

Then go home and drink a hot cup of tea.
Then go home and drink a hot cup of tea!
And when life gets rough
Know that you'll be tough
Because you've learned from Charlotte of the sea!